Rejected From The Womb,

But Chosen By GOD

Rejected From The Womb, But Chosen By GOD

Dorothy Elaine Davis (Mc Leod)

authorHOUSE®

AuthorHouse™
1663 Liberty Drive
Bloomington, IN 47403
www.authorhouse.com
Phone: 1-800-839-8640

First published by AuthorHouse   06/21/2011

ISBN: 978-1-4634-2603-3 (sc)
ISBN: 978-1-4634-2602-6 (ebk)

Library of Congress Control Number: 2011910631

Printed in the United States of America

Any people depicted in stock imagery provided by Thinkstock are models, and such images are being used for illustrative purposes only.
Certain stock imagery © Thinkstock.

This book is printed on acid-free paper.

Contents

Dedication

This book is dedicated to http://www.churchofgodbibletruth.com. I have much to be thankful for, because of the opportunity given to write this book. Bible Truth ministry gave me a lot of hope. I think it's interesting that I was baptized in 1975 but only began to understand the Word of God in 2006. I attended many churches but was unable to stay focused on the preaching, because I was so distressed from coping with everyday life—trying to provide food and clothes for my children and sending them to school. My husband was not much of a provider. At times, I felt like I was a man, having to take on the harder things. Since our relationship began, I was the one who provided shelter, and it had been that way since he left his mother's house.

I loved the Lord Jesus Christ, but I was unable to understand the Word of God, so I resorted to reading the psalms of David as a prayer. I feared God, and reading the psalms helped me to shun the things that were evil, such as witchcraft, prostitution, and theft. Because I had the children to support and didn't have any help, I took on work like washing for people or selling things. I wasn't bringing in enough money to pay one-tenth for tithes, because of the great expense of supporting six children. Sometimes I didn't have any job at all.

Because of the financial trouble I was having, I believed I was cursed and felt like I was robbing God, like most preachers would teach. Sometimes when I went to church, I felt ashamed, because I wasn't able to give an offering. There were times I couldn't go to church, because I felt like the clothes I had were too shabby. So, I continued to resort to looking up toward the sky and praying to the Lord.

I toiled through a lot of isolation and embarrassing moments to obtain food for my children. My husband always had a little job but nothing that would bring much pay, and he also refused to give me much. He became involved in drinking alcohol and getting himself drunk, and then he would physically abuse me in the presence of the children.

There were times in Jamaica when I stumbled to attend a crusade, hoping the minister would call me up like the others and lay hands on me. I believed that this would change my life and situation, but I wasn't fortunate. After moving to the Cayman Islands, I miraculously found Bible Truth ministry, and it was there I began to read and understand the word of God. I became distracted from my problems, and the word of God became a total deliverance for me. Because of my experience, I would encourage the readers to spend quality time reading the word of God. I was set free by doing so. I received the knowledge and understanding that I had needed so badly. It transformed my life and enabled me to reach the place where I could put this story in writing—*Rejected from the Womb but Chosen by God.*

Acknowledgments

This book would not have been possible without the Lord Jesus Christ and the support and encouragement of my son, Andre Oliver Davis; son-in-law, John David Ebanks; daughters, Ruth Jacqueline Ebanks, and Karen Elizabeth Davis; husband, Norman Anthony Davis; and grandson, Joseph Joshua Anthony Bodden. In the process of writing my story, I have come to realize that I was truly chosen by God to survive so many rejections, abuse, mental breakdowns, and obstacles. There were also many friends who gave me much encouragement from time to time. They have been there like family, taking the place of sisters, brothers, and mother.

I was encouraged by the word of God, knowing He cared for the fatherless. I also took courage and great pride, working hard and not refusing any kind of job to put food in my children's mouth. Yes, I had to walk from church to church, many times knocking on their doors to beg for food. There were some who helped, such as Pastor Bobby Wilmot and Reverend Neil. My cousin Oswald Mc Leod was also an important force in my life, standing with me like a big brother and encouraging me to believe in myself. There were some pastors who responded with such a cold heart, and had I not know God personally, I would have given up. But I heard the still small voice of the Lord Jesus telling me to trust Him, which made me confident in Jesus Christ.

I encouraged myself through the words of the psalmist David: Psalms 23, 27, 91, and 107. There were times when I felt like a failure to my children and my husband, who was unable to love me for reasons I still don't know up till today. It's in writing this book that I realize I was trapped in my own fear due to the constant abuses.

Preface

This story is true, and I would like to say that after getting to know my mother, Rebecca Bernard I found out she was a loving and good woman. She assisted her sisters by helping them raise their children. She also took many children off the street in Kingston, Jamaica. She was very hard working, and despite her rejection, I was still proud to have been her daughter. She was a very beautiful woman who was half Indian, with hair long reaching her buttocks. But she was hurt and betrayed when she found out that my father was married.

After I became an adult, I could understand and see much clearer. I don't think she was hurt or affected by her actions. She said that at the time she got pregnant, she had just received an opportunity for a job in Canada.

I couldn't hate her, and so I was hurt to know that she was unable to love me. I couldn't turn back the clock of her disappointment, so I kept dreaming of her forgiveness. She couldn't forgive me until three days before she passed away. At that time, she also told me that she didn't send me any barrels or clothes like she did for the others because I was more hardworking, independent, and determined to get the things I needed, while the rest were more in need of her. I forgave her, because looking on the situation one mother to another, I understood.

Dorothy Elaine Davis (Mc Leod)

I knew my mother and siblings when I was thirteen years old and thought the situation was awkward and sudden for all of us. No one sought any kind of counseling. That's not to say that a counselor can solve problems, but no one got the chance to speak about how they felt. My father didn't say much about the incident with my mother putting me on the sidewalk. He thought he was protecting me from feeling embarrassed or hurt. He would always say that my mother was pretty, and I could tell he was attracted to her and seemed to have loved her then. My aunt, Inez Mc Leod, and stepmother, Olive Mc Leod, were the ones who really told me the story, and there are persons who are still alive who knew about it.

I didn't hate my mother. I never had the heart to, and after becoming a mother, I realized a lot. But one thing I pledged was to never give away any of my children. I challenged the hardship, fighting for life. I never bothered my mother for any help for my children, who grew up without the experience of having a grandmother. My sisters were more privileged to have had a mother to be there for them, and their children had a grandmother to send barrels of clothes, money, and other things. She went all out for my siblings, while I went all out for my children, putting food on the table and a roof over their heads.

Some of my children might feel I didn't do enough, and this is one of the reasons I am writing this book. I know deep in my heart that I did the best I could. I am not making excuses or saying things were great for them, but I had an abusive husband to live with, one who couldn't show me any love. I worked for his love, but it wasn't enough. He made me believe that because I was a dark-skinned woman, I was not beautiful. My husband told me things that made me feel something was so wrong that no one would love me.

He said no one would love or want me, because I had too many children—five of whom I'd had with him. He only loved to have sex with me, and that was all he was interested in. He would describe me as stink, and he scorned me. He would just have sex, and as he got up, he was ready to curse me. I was afraid to leave him, because he threatened to kill me. I was trapped in my fears and felt rejected by one I loved. I am writing this, so the reader will understand the story—my story.

Chapter 1

REJECTED FROM THE WOMB

My mother rejected me from the womb, because she found out early in her pregnancy that my father was a married man. She felt betrayed and bitter. My father is Cecil Luriel Mc Leod. He was an ex-soldier and electrical engineer in the Jamaican Regiment, leader of the Jamaica Military Band, and member of the Royal Air Force. He went to World War II, and afterward, he went to be a warder at the General Penitentiary in Kingston, Jamaica.

At that time, the prisons often requested high-ranking soldiers to work. It was during that time my father and mother formed a relationship. Back then in Jamaica, some women were attracted to and very excited about uniformed men, such as policemen, soldiers, and firemen. Other features women were drawn to included tall and handsome, whether white, brown, or black. My father was one of the tall, black, and handsome uniformed men. He was always neatly attired, he wore a gold crown on one of his front teeth, and when he was not in uniform, he wore the most expensive clothes. He also walked with a cane to spice up his dress code and loved wearing expensive felt hats.

My mother was bitter and angry and felt betrayed. She then decided to take the matter further by trying to abort me in order to get rid of her problem. She began drinking all kinds of concoctions, but she was unsuccessful in her plight, which left her no choice but to carry the pregnancy to term and give birth.

Chapter 2

MY MOTHER

I was my mother's second child and second daughter. She had left her first daughter Shella Anderson in Tollgate district clarendon parish to be raised by one of her sister Ivy Baker.

In those days, most men would wait until the child was born before taking any responsibility. The child would have to resemble of the father to pass the test. Some men went to the extreme and said that if the baby wasn't a son, they would not claim the child.

When I was born, I looked extremely white. My skin tone was caused by the things my mother drank to end the pregnancy. I was also born without any hair on my head.

My father was a black man there is no way he would have accepted me to be his child after seeing me. However, he wanted a child, because he'd had a son who had died when he was only four years old. Even though he was married and having an affair with my mother, he took responsibility of paying my mother's rent and helped her out in other ways. My father's sister, Inez Mc Leod, lived next door to my Mother in Rae Town. My father lived with

3

his wife, Olive Mc Leod, in Mountain View, which was a good distance away. It was convenient for him to visit my mother, because he worked at the General Penitentiary located in Ray Town.

Chapter 3

RAE TOWN

Rae Town was the center Parish of Kingston, which is home to quite a few historic places. Rae Town was full of life and close to quite a few general markets. Popular locations included Caimans, Cremo Ice Cream Company (Jamaica's first ice company), and the Molasses Factory. Then there was the Myrtle Bank Hotel, which was not so far away. There are also a lot of wharves. The first home of Jamaica, Gleaner Company. All of these were located on Harbor Street. There was also the Salvation Army Church on Tower Street. Every Sunday evening they would dress up in their army-looking outfits and come out with their marching band. People of all ages would come out on the road or look through their windows to see and hear them as they played.

Mutabaruka, the great Jamaican poet, was also born in Rae Town. And then there were the Jonkanoos—people who dressed up in animal costumes. There was one who dressed as the devil and held a long fork. A lot of children were afraid of them. I was afraid of that one with the long fork.

Most of the men who lived in Rae Town loved the sea and were good swimmers. They also loved to fish. People would wake up early in the morning to get a sea bath. In those times, there were no fridges, so people would buy ice from old men who pushed carts filled with ice through the town. There were also a lot of little restaurants, which were called cold supper shops. They would have showcases and display all the traditional Jamaican food, such as corn meal pudding, potato pudding, escubiched saltfish fritters, blue draws, and the refreshing ginger beer, not to mention that there were a lot of rum bars.

Chapter 4

DEPRIVED FROM
BEING BREASTFED

After my mother gave birth on May 3rd, 1952, she refused to breastfeed me or even allow me to suckle at her breast. Not only was she angry about finding out that my father was married, but she was also upset by the fact that he disowned me, which most of his friends and colleagues encouraged him to do.

My mother was half Indian—her mother was Jamaican, and her father was Indian by birth, hailing from New Deli. My Aunt Inez had no children. One day my mother placed me in a cardboard box and set me on the sidewalk near my Aunt Inez's gate. I was only three weeks old. My aunt took me off the street and pledged to raise me as her own child. She gave me the pet name Pepper, because I cried a lot. Luckily, she didn't live far from the seaside, and she would take me for walks there to help me sleep.

My aunt was a jack of many trades. She worked as a part-time chef at the Myrtle Bank Hotel, which was located on Harbor Street in Kingston. She owned two restaurants and was also a sidewalk curio vender. She sold a variety of craft items made from straw, such as baskets hats, handbags, purses, belts, and slippers.

She would take me with her when she sold curios and keep me in a cardboard box by the roadside, but I got the best care. In those days, the tourist ships would dock at the Wharves Harbor Street, so we'd have tourists and sailors going to and fro. Some of these visitors would take a picture of me sitting in the box on the sidewalk.

My dad would come by and look for my aunt from time to time. My mother moved on with her life quickly, as if everything were normal—like she'd gotten rid of her biggest problem. But as time went by, my skin color began changing and getting darker. Both my aunt and father noticed the change. By the time I reached a year old, I was the living resemblance of my father. Because of the change, my father didn't hold back and started supporting me financially. He began to boast to his friends and colleagues about his daughter.

I was fed with all kinds of tin feeding and milk formulas to replace the breast milk. When I turned two years old, I began to break out with sores all over my body. At one time, it got so bad that the sores covered me from head to toe. The doctors said the condition was a result of the different milk formulas I was fed. At that time although my mother was living next door, she never even looked over the fence at me, so my aunt and father were all I had.

My father's wife was very upset with him, but she was unable to have children, and my father wanted children. He was happy knowing I was his, but my stepmother came up with a plan out of fear. She felt insecure and thought that my father might get back together with my mother, because she lived so close. She knew he was visiting more regularly, so she began to encourage him to take me from my aunt. That way, they could both would raise me together. My Aunt Inez was not happy about it, because she was the one who had saved me by taking me off the sidewalk. She felt my father was being ungrateful.

My father wanted me to have a better, stable life, and he thought the only way to do that was to have me at his home. He had built a two-bedroom house on a large piece of leased land and believed that was best for me.

My aunt then gave the matter thought and agreed.

Chapter 5

LIVING WITH MY FATHER

When I was three years old, my father took me home to live with him and his wife. After he took me from my aunt, he stopped visiting my aunt often. He was upset with what my mother had done by putting me on the sidewalk. He came home after work as early as he possible could.

My Aunt Inez would come to visit me and bring me pretty dresses. At Christmastime, she took me to the grand markets. She remembered all of my birthdays and bought me lots of toys, dolls, and accessories to use with my dolly house.

When I was like six years old and there was moonlight, the children in Jamaica played different ring games, where we would clap hands and sing folk songs, like those that Jamaican Louse Benet wrote. I loved playing with my dolly house. I had started calling my aunt Mama. My father was highly looked up to in his community, because he'd done well in the army and with his job being a warder at the General Penitentiary. He received the last of many medals August 6, 1962, for efficiency in service. He was exceptional at his job. He was responsible for the first electrical installation of the Rock Fort Mineral Bath in Kingston and received all kinds of medals and promotions.

My stepmother seemed to have one face in front of my father and another face behind his back. I was treated with so much remorse. My stepmother took out her anger about my mother coming into her marriage on me, and I was paying the price. Her resentment toward me was so bad at times that she'd tell me nothing good would come out of me. My father had no idea, and I didn't say a word to him about what was happening. My father treated me like a little princess, and I wasn't lacking anything. He saw to it that I had everything—the best clothes, shoes, and food—and he leave no stone unturned.

I began attending school when I was three years old. I went to one of the best and most expensive prep schools on Sligo Road off Mountain View, Kingston. I can remember clearly a classmate, Althea Mc Cray, who became the post mistress for Maggoty Post Office in St. Elizabeth, Jamaica. Most of the children attending had parents who were nurses, doctors, soldiers, or policemen. I felt quite okay knowing my father was a big warder and an ex-soldier. I felt special and interacted with any grade or color of person. My father treated me like a son, taking me to cricket matches, ring-side boxing, football games, and bingo parties. My stepmother didn't love going out. I didn't tell my father the things my stepmother did to me; instead, I told him the opposite.

I can remember singing at school concerts from the age of five, and people would ask me to sing more songs. My father made it his duty to be there, supporting and clapping for me. He would take me home on his back—we called it a donkey ride. I was all dressed up with colored ribbons to match my dress and silver earrings. My stepmother was very proud of me, despite the fact that she wasn't nice. But she was insecure that when I grew old enough I would go to my mother. This was nowhere in my mind.

Sometimes my stepmother's friends would come over hungry, and she would give them food. My father, who was very strict about who came to his home, didn't know about this. I didn't say a word to him, but I would give my dinner to anyone who came and was hungry.

In the mornings I always left breakfast for a little girl named Grace. Her parents didn't like me, but Grace liked me, and I liked her too. Gracey still lived in Mountain View, Kingston. When my dad came home from work, he would bring me all kinds of goodies—chocolate, peanuts, popcorn, candy, and more. I shared with the less fortunate children who lived nearby. My father didn't want me to become friends with these children, but when he found out I was sharing my goodies, he brought extra, so I could share and still have some left for myself.

A prisoner who was serving a life sentence at the prison where my father worked made me a savings box for my ninth birthday. Every month my father gave me an allowance. I didn't have to spend my money to buy anything, because I didn't have a need to, so I saved it in my little box. There were times when someone would come to our house in need, and my stepmother would come to me and ask me to lend them some money. I was more than happy to help.

My father restrained me from doing housework and made it clear that he wanted me to study hard, because he wanted me to become a maternity nurse, which is the same thing as a midwife. He had sisters who were maternity nurses and many other family members who were in the nursing profession. Because nursing was a highly professional job, I had to take my schoolwork seriously. Every evening when he came home from work, I had to show him my work. If I got an x, I received a beating. Every time my father asked me to do something, such as going to the store, he looked at his watch and told me what time I should be back. He was strict and sending me a message of not spoiling me, kind of making me be on time, saying that I shouldn't stop to play when I was send out—so it was about scolding me. When his rule was broken, I received a beating. I was so afraid of the beatings that I would lie about things. Things could not have been better. My father made sure I was registered to have a birth certificate and gave me all my names. Dorothy Elaine. I also received all of my vaccinations, which my mother knew nothing about.

Chapter 6

MY COMFORT ZONE CRUMBLED

In November 1962, at the age of eleven, my comfortable world was shattered. One morning I woke up very early and noticed my father's watch on the dresser. I became curious as to why it was there that time of the morning. My stepmother was still sound asleep, so I got up and began searching all around for my father.

It was about five o'clock in the morning and was still dark. I opened the door and went outside, but I didn't see or hear him. Before leaving the house, I noticed that his shoes and uniform were still at their usual place. That left me no choice but to go outside and look to see if he was outside. I didn't remember him saying he wasn't going to work, and he usually shared things like that with me. I then checked the bathroom outside and decided to knock on the door, thinking he was inside using it. I knocked about three times, but there was no answer.

I pushed the door open and saw him in a sitting position on the bathroom floor. His head was hanging down, and he looked like he was sleeping. I called him, "Papa, Papa, Papa," and he began to make a funny sound. It sounded like he was struggling to answer me. I ran to wake up my stepmother and woke the whole neighborhood up as I cried out, "My father is dead. My father is dead." Then, two of my father's coworkers, one Mr. Lindoe and Mr. Chang, who lived close by came to the rescue and took him to the hospital. I also went to the hospital and sat in the hallway, crying my eyes out. There were several doctors around him, and after a while, one of them came out and said they tried their best to save his life, but he had died. They couldn't find the reason or cause. It was then and there that my comfort zone was shattered. I became empty and alone.

My stepmother's friends came and were there for her, but they didn't pay much attention to me. It was my Aunt Inez who came and comforted me, also my little friends who I used to share my candies and goodies with.

At only eleven years old, I was the one who had to explain what I had seen when my father died. I had to give personal information about him, because my stepmother couldn't read or write. I had to be in charge. He received a state funeral with a marching procession and gun salute because he was an ex-soldier.

My stepmother's friends didn't waste any time telling her to send me to my mother. My allowance, which I had saved in the little box, went to purchase gloves for his burial. That was when my stepmother stood up for me. She assured me that she wouldn't send me to my mother, because I had to be her right hand and to inform the lawyers of where my father's assets where—he had confided in me.

All of this time, I didn't see or hear from my mother. Everyone thought that she must have heard about my father's death, because it was announced on the radio and gleaner. My stepmother continued sending me to school, and when I became twelve, I began going to

Vauxhall Secondary School and continued to excel in my schoolwork.

My father's estate took a long time to process, because he didn't have a will. However, my stepmother sent me to school out of her widow's mite.

Chapter 7

MEETING MY MOTHER
FOR THE FIRST TIME

When I was thirteen years old, one Sunday evening while I was ironing my uniform, I heard a knock on the gate. I went to see who was knocking and what they wanted. I saw a young, beautiful Indian woman who looked like she was in her thirties. I asked if I could help her, not knowing who she was. She explained that she was my mother. I stood there in shock, not knowing what to do or think.

I called to my stepmother, who came see what was going on. Again, the woman said she was my mother. My stepmother invited her in, and they began talking about my father, among other things. My mother wanted to know which school I was attending, and my stepmother gave her all the information. I looked outside to the road and saw a green station wagon. In it sat a middle-aged white man, who was my mother's common-law-husband.

My mother didn't say much to me, and when she left, there were no hugs or any kind of comfort to me. She was more interested in getting some information. My stepmother contacted my Aunt Inez and told her about my mother's visit. She was very upset and wondered what my mother was really up to. It caused a great concern in the community, because since I had started living there, no one knew of my mother or ever saw her. I had mixed feelings. A part of me was glad to see her, and a part of me wasn't quite sure how to feel.

One day after school, my mother turned up when school dismissed. She recognized me, asking for me by name. She explained that she was going to take me to meet my siblings. I hesitated, because I knew my stepmother knew nothing about it and would be looking to see me come home from school. I pointed this out to her, but she said to me she would bring me back when we were done. I had no choice, as she demanded that I go with her. Again, her common-law-husband was driving the same green car. I went with her.

Chapter 8

TAKEN AGAINST MY WISH

When we got to her house, she told the children there that I was their sister. There were three girls and two boys. These, she said, were my siblings. I didn't quite know how to act, as everything was happening so fast.

I was the eldest sibling. At that moment, my older sister Shella was living in Toll Gate Clarendon and being raised by my mother's sister, Ivy Baker. My mother and her common-law-husband left and told me they would be back soon to take me home. The house was a mess, and she asked me to do some cleaning. I was not accustomed to cleaning, but I tried and messed up my uniform.

I didn't feel any kind of connection with my siblings. They didn't care about me being there. They were just glad our mother was gone, so they could continue playing. I noticed that it was getting late. Night was coming down, and I was concerned that my stepmother would be worried, because she didn't know where I was.

There was no telephone at the house. My mother came home very late and told me that she would take me home the following day. I explained to her that I had to attend school and that I wasn't used to skipping school. At that time, only my two white sisters were attending school. My black sister and two brothers weren't attending school. I also said that I couldn't sleep the night, because I was worried about my stepmother.

The next day my mother made no attempt to take me home but continued making excuses saying that she wasn't going to take me home the next day. I missed school quite a few days, and when I went back, my teachers were very concerned. They asked where I had been, because my stepmother was investigating my whereabouts. My stepmother didn't know where I was, she went to the police station, but was told she would have to wait for a few days to make a missing report. My mother insisted on taking me back to her house, claiming she was my mother, and she was calling the shots—in other words, I should shut up. I didn't say anything out of fear to my teachers about what was going on, with my mother forcing me to stay with her.

I didn't want to stay with her, because I wasn't ready to be with her. I called my father's house home, but at her house, I was a stranger among my siblings. I wasn't interested in connecting with my siblings. I grew up by myself, and I had friends plus everything to make me comfortable. I didn't have any need or desire to be where I had to share my space. I didn't feel like I belonged there.

I was not interested in my mother, and I didn't want to live with her and her common-law-husband. To me, it was too soon, and also I felt obligated to stay with my stepmother and be there with her, because she was there for me. I never wanted to live with my mother, which would have made me seem ungrateful. My father was gone, and I wanted to stay where he left me, but my mother forced me to stay with her. While I was there, I was not going to school regularly, because I was made to do housework. I was questioned by my mother about my father's estate and other private matters.

I protected my stepmother. I had an uncle, Edward Mc Leod, one of my father's brothers, who was an inspector of police. He kind of took the place of my father and was also assisting with the distribution of my father's estate. I couldn't reach him, and my mother made sure that she was at the school before it even dismissed, so I couldn't get away. My aunt knew where my mother worked and went there to fight.

My mother called the police, so my aunt left. My mother had me direct her to where my uncle was living; she had never met him up to this point. My mother's plan was to find out how much money was being left for me and to make things look as if I was in her care. She, being my mother, would have to be the one to in control of whatever money was coming to me. What my mother didn't know is that this Uncle Edward knew about how she had put me on the sidewalk. When we arrived at my uncle's house, I quickly relayed the matter to him, and he chased her away and took me back home to my stepmother.

When we got home, I told them all that had happened to me. The incident affected me, and I was scared that she might come again to take me. My stepmother was also concerned, especially in the afternoons. At this time, my stepmother hadn't gotten any of my father's money, so she was still supporting me out of her widow's mite. There were times the food was not enough, and she would give what there was to me and not eat any herself. I would lie to her and tell her my belly was full, so she would eat too. She continued caring for me just as much as my father did, and by this time, her friends were on our side and against what my mother was trying to do.

However, I wasn't entitled to any of my father's money, because I was considered a bastard child. When my stepmother got the money, she put it all in Barkley's bank and gave me access to withdraw money for both our needs. My aunt also went ahead and took out an insurance policy with British Insurance Company, located then on Harbour Street, Kingston for me, so when I left school, I could start up a business. She suggested a restaurant, because that was one kind of business she use to do. All of this time I still called her Mama, and she was always there for me.

My Aunt Inez and stepmother, Olive, agreed that I could visit my mother, but I never liked visiting my mother. She always asked so many questions about my stepmother's private business. I didn't provide her with the information or speak badly about my stepmother. My mother wanted me to stay with her, but then I would miss school and have to do her housework, which I didn't like doing.

My aunt was trying to encourage me to have a relationship with her, because my father had passed away. She even gave my mother an opportunity to help me by placing my insurance policy in her hand, so she could assist in paying half of the premium. My mother never paid anything on it, but in no time, she began to take out loans on the policy, and it became bankrupt. No one knew then—not even me. I was always excelling and doing well in school, but my mother's interference affected me. She wasn't loving or affectionate toward me and would make negative remarks about my hair not being as straight as the others' hair. She treated me more like a helper than a daughter.

My mother insisted that I stay with her and visit my stepmother. Again, my world was turned upside down, but I had no choice. So, I stayed for a while. She and her common-law-husband owned their own business. He was from England and had no relatives in or from Jamaica. He was a very interesting man with many skills. He had come to Jamaica as an engineer to work on ships, he had a lot of equipment that was used to make things, such as white lime, asphalt, putty, and sea let soap powder. He also had a hardware store named Windward Hardware.

My mother often worked there to help him, and they also had a cashier and a delivery driver. My mother was hard working, and her common-law-husband provided her with a good life. She had a part-time helper. My sisters were crazy when my mother and her husband were at work—they would turn on all the pipes and leave the water running, they trained the dogs to sit and eat around the table, they dressed up the dogs in clothes and put them in the bath, and they would call people on the phone and curse them. Everyone was crazy, and I was worried. When my mother came home, it wouldn't matter if me or my other black sister, Elaine, did something wrong, but we would get the blame. According to her, we were the bigger ones and shouldn't let it happen.

My white brother would hide under the fence and use the water hose to spray people who passed by on the road. One evening a lady came and knocked on the gate to complain about it. All of us were inside the house listening and peeping through the window, worried sick. We heard when our mother asked the woman to get away from her gate, as if she didn't accept the complaint about my brother wetting anyone. We were all happy, thinking we had avoided a beating. But when she came inside, we heard her ask my little sister to get the belt. We all received beatings. It didn't matter who did it. I was fed up of this treatment, because every evening when she came home, there was always something. On the other hand, her husband wasn't too quick to beat the girls like she was.

One Sunday evening my mother put a large piece of roast beef on the dining table. One of the dogs named Worrie saw it, went around the table, and took and ate the beef. My mother and her husband were just in time to catch the dog; neither my siblings nor myself could say anything, because we knew the dog wasn't stealing but had been taught to eat around the table. My mother and her husband decided to shoot the dog. We were all devastated, because we loved that dog so much, but no one could say anything.

I wasn't happy living with my mother. I thought her husband was a good man, but I didn't get along with her. I wasn't going to school as regularly as I use to, she eventually fired her helper, and my black sister and I were supposed to take her place.

I was unable to cope. She was abusive to me, and she blamed everything that happened in the house on me. I could hardly sit down and watch the television, because she was constantly calling me to do something. I even had to light her cigarettes. She was a hard smoker, using one cigarette to light the other. So, I decided to run away to my aunt's house. This was a different aunt, but also a sister of my father, Aunt Whillel Mc Leod. Not long after I arrived at my aunt's, my mother came with the police during the night (she had paid them), and they told my aunt to return me. When I arrived back at her house, she increased the abuse, and I was treated like a slave.

I decided to run away again to Aunt Inez's house, and, again, she came with police, who she paid. They told my aunt to return me. I told myself I would be on the run again. The last time I ran away I went back to my stepmother, who went to the cops. This time, the cops told her to go home and take me, and she shouldn't worry. They told her if and when my mother came back, she should come and report her. Even though she was my mother, my stepmother was also my legal guardian. My mother didn't come after me this time, but I lived in fear.

I then got involved with a boy named Trevor Bernard, who was fourteen years of age like myself too. He told me he loved me and said I was beautiful. This was the first person to tell me he loved me since my father passed on. This relationship helped me to recover from the way my mother made me feel like I was ugly. My father used to tell me I was beautiful.

Trevor was my first boyfriend, but neither my stepmother nor mother had ever sat me down to tell me anything about my period, menstruation, or pregnancy. They said nothing. When my first period came, I was so frightened, because I thought something bad had happen to me to cause the bleeding. I quickly told one of my friends who explained that nothing bad was happening. I was just menstruating. I was so happy to know that nothing was wrong with me that I start shouting, "I am menstruating!" When my stepmother heard me, she quickly called me, investigated the matter, and told me not to shout it out. She said it should be a secret, but back in those days, there weren't many sanitary napkins around. People would use white cloth that had been cut into pieces and folded. After the period finished, we would wash them out and put them up for the next month. I never shared this with my mother, and she didn't ask me if I had started menstruating while I was with her.

Her common-law-husband was the one who told me about boys and sex. He told me that I was a beautiful black girl and that I was pretty, but my mother said the opposite. She would complain about the texture of my hair. She gave me a sense of a low self-esteem about my personality, as if being black was bad. She did the same thing to my sister Elaine. She was treated like a servant, and we were called nicknames of the worse sort, like Congo and Paney. I noticed that my sister didn't speak much. She wasn't sent to school much and was treated like the helper by our mother.

I decided that if I was going to be in involved in sex, it would be Trevor, who had said that he loved me. Trevor wasn't joking; he really loved me. A lot of girls wanted to be with him. I remember writing him a little love letter. He wasted no time responding.

He didn't need to hide from his mother in order to talk to me, because he told her that he loved me. On my side of the fence, however, I had to hide in order to talk to him. One evening a friend had asked me to do some babysitting. I didn't know she had a plan to tell Trevor I called and lure him to come see me at the house where I was staying with her baby. As soon as he came over, my friend took the child and proceeded to call my stepmother, unknown to us.

We were hugging and kissing, and yes, we began to take things further than they should have been. I was also vulnerable and was feeling a need for affection and love, because I was really missing my father. I ended up having sex with the boy, when, all of a sudden, the door was flung open with rage. It was my stepmother. My boyfriend was so frightened that he ran out of the house, while my stepmother dragged me and hauled me out. She made such a scene that a crowd came, and some were laughing. That was my first time having sex, and it was with a boy I had loved and who loved me too. My stepmother hauled me on the road where a crowd followed and took me to the police station, as if I were a criminal, and beat me. The police didn't act, as if she were doing the right thing. I was so humiliated. On the next day of school, the news had reached the other students, and I was mocked and called names. Some children approached me, wanting to pick a fight. I began to feel that sex was a bad thing.

Chapter 9

PREGNANT AT FOURTEEN YEARS OLD

Three months after I hadn't had any period, my stepmother took me to the University Hospital where we found out I was pregnant. I was fourteen years old. My stepmother was furious; she cursed me at the hospital, on the road, in the bus, and right until we got home. My stepmother was someone who spoke about sex only in a negative way. She was unable to read and write and described sex to be dirty and nasty, and it was all bad.

I had just taken my technical school examination, and my teachers were very confident I would pass it. This exam was to give me the opportunity to attend a technical high school. I can remember hiding in the house for the entire nine months of the pregnancy. The only time I came out was to go to and bathroom, which was outside. I would cover up myself with a big sheet, so no one could see me. I felt so dirty, like a criminal, and I treated myself as such.

When it was time for me to attend clinic, my stepmother would wake up in the darkest part of the morning. She was ashamed of me and didn't want anyone to see us. It was like I was serving a sentence for a crime. Her friends advised her to abort the pregnancy and make me continue school, seeing I was so bright and doing well. In those days, abortions were performed by people boiling up some sort of concoction that the woman would then drink to get rid of the pregnancy. There was a fifty-fifty chance that it would work, but she refused to do it. When my mother heard the news, she told me to go to the police and tell them I was raped. She wanted them to arrest the boy, because I was considered underage. I didn't do that, though, because I knew it would be a lie. The pregnancy was caused by having sex with my boyfriend one time. He owned the pregnancy, but he wasn't out of school yet. He was still a teenager too.

His parents were doing fairly well, and he was their only son—an heir. His family wasn't short of finance, and his mother didn't argue, because he told her that he loved me. I wasn't seen as the worst person. His parents knew my father and had looked up to him.

The daughter of one of my stepmother's friends—the one who set us up that night—was filled with envy and thought he was too good for me. She went to my boyfriend's mother and told her that they should wait until the child was born to see if it was his. My stepmother became very upset about the matter and refused help from the family. Instead, she took money from what my father had left, which was a good sum, to help finance the pregnancy. I ate the best food, wore the best maternity clothes, and didn't want for anything. My mother came a few times with a little food, but my stepmother handled all the expenses and made sure I attended my monthly clinic at the University Hospital, which was and still is considered to be the best material hospital in Jamaica My Aunt Inez also assisted. She never quarreled with me but was quite understanding and encouraged me with what I could do after I had the child, like find an evening class. When I turned eighteen, she said

I could open a restaurant with the insurance money she had taken out. She was paying all of it, even when she placed it in my mother's care. After I had my child, a son named Michael, we found out I had passed my exams, but I was unable to attend the high school, because I was a mother.

Chapter 10

I GOT A JOB

I decided to find a job. I was bright and fairly intelligent. My stepmother gave up and decided she wouldn't spend any more money. My mother was no encouragement, but at one time, she asked me what kind of classes I would like to attend. I told her I would like to learn how to be a receptionist. She discouraged me and suggested that I go learn dressmaking. I didn't like the idea, but I didn't argue.

Her common-law husband took me somewhere to enroll in dressmaking, but that was it. They never went back, so I went and found a job working for a white Englishman at his pen factory. I worked assembling pens. The man I worked for was also one of the owners of Woolworths. He helped me believe in myself, and I earned some good money. At the time, my stepmother bought everything my son Michael, whose pet name was Bunny, needed; it was as if she didn't want me to do anything for him.

When I took my son to see my siblings, my white sisters were crazy and treated him like a dolly. Each one gave him a bath, one after the other. I don't think my mother loved him, seeing he had such strong Indian features.

I remember one day I took my son to the store to purchase a pair of shoes. My son was very brown and looked more like an Indian boy. I took him to the store, which was owned by some Syrians, and put set him down in a chair. When I came to pick him up, the manager of the store, probably seeing me as a black girl, came to me in defensive way and asked why I was taking the child. I explained that he was my son. The manager then gave me a discount and told me to come back; it was like he was giving me a gift for having a little boy like this. My stepmother showed him off as if he were her child.

My job at the pen factory was going well, but my stepmother broke up the relationship with my baby's father Trevor and placed a restriction on the child. Trevor wasn't allowed to see his child, and I couldn't talk to him. So, we broke it off for good. His mother took it in the sense that Olive, my stepmother, didn't like Trevor, so she advised him to keep his distance. But he was still protective of me and still said he loved me. We never had sex again; it was only just that one time. He felt bad about everything that happened to me and was concerned how my stepmother treated me. No one could do anything to me, because he would quickly come to my defense.

My stepmother became so possessive of Michael that she began to act as if she were his mother. She even went as far as to give him her breast, which had no milk. She began to show me so much hatefulness and resentfulness. She wanted to drive me out of the house, so it would seem that I wasn't his mother but his sister. She took it on herself to go register my son in my father's name, Michael Mc Leod, instead of his father's surname, Bernard.

I made myself independent, working and trying to put up with everything. I told myself that I was going to stay right there at my daddy's house. My aunt always encouraged me. I can remember going to my mother's workplace, only to discover that she had migrated to Canada. Yes, at that point, I had to face the facts of life—I was very much alone and felt like an orphan.

When I turned eighteen, I decided to go check on my insurance money to see if I could collect it and open up a restaurant. I picked out a building and had it all planned, only to discover that my mother had borrowed all of my money, and there was nothing to collect. The workers at the insurance office felt sorry for me, and they came and comforted me. I was really crying hard, and they told me that my mother had borrowed the money to purchase school books for my half sisters. I was in a total mess, because I had my mind all set on this money to start my little restaurant. I still loved my son's father but was forbidden to see him.

Chapter 11

MY SECOND BOYFRIEND

At sixteen years old, I met a man Nemiah Brown who I formed a friendship with, and he was kind to me. I was still living at my father's house, and this man, who had his own rented place, was living in the same community that I lived in. He came from the parish of St. Ann, Jamaica, so he would be referred to as a country man. I was a town girl, being born in Kingston, which is the capital of Jamaica. He was a carpenter by profession and made furniture. He also did roofing and worked for Remars Furnishing Company, located on Orange Street, downtown Kingston. He was five years older than me.

Soon, things became more serious, and we began an intimate relationship. My stepmother didn't have any problem with him, because she was so caught up with acting like my son's mother. Nemiah was very caring and kind to me, and he invited me to meet his parents, living in St. Ann's Parish, who accepted me. The people in the country respond to me as being a pretty girl. And they showed much love; in the country, everyone addresses one other as family.

When my son was two years old, I became pregnant with my second child. Nemiah treated me like a queen—he never made me do anything, he washed my clothes, he cooked, and he never lifted his hand to hit me. The people in the country loved me. I began to feel like I was cared for and wanted, like I felt when my father was alive, but I didn't like the country much.

At the time my second baby was due, it was common for mothers to have their children at home, which was called home delivery. Nemiah had to gather lots of wood so he could make a fire to boil water for the occasion. When my labor pains began, he went for the midwife, who lived several miles away. She rode a donkey to come to our home. That same night there was another woman who was also having labor pains and had need for the midwife, but my baby's father was the first to reach her. The other mother then began to have problems and was rushed off to the hospital.

I was also having difficulties, and my daughter was unable to be born. I became so scared, because in those times, a lot of mothers died during childbirth. The old midwife was a Christian, spiritual woman and believed that a big crack in the wall was causing the problems I was having. She spoke a kind of spiritual language; she was loud and blunt. I had my Bible open and was reading Psalms 143. Nemiah loved reading his Bible. The midwife told me to get on my knees, and it was then that my daughter was born. This was Nemiah's first child; we decided to call her Princess.

After the birth, my baby's father didn't make his sisters or mother come to do anything. He took care of the cleaning up and everything else. When the child was three months old, we decided to take her to see my stepmother, who immediately called her the name Dawn, because she was born at the dawn of the morning. I stayed there a few months, while he stayed with some friends. Again, my stepmother wanted to take my daughter away, but her father Nemiah wouldn't allow it. Olive my stepmother made sure that she held on to my son Michael a little more. I wasn't allowed to talk to or even hold my son, but he did love me. He would hide and come to me when she wasn't looking.

After a few months, we went back to the country. When my daughter was three months old, I became pregnant with my third child at age seventeen. My baby's father, Nemiah, continued taking the best care of me. My third child, a son named Aaron, was also born at home. Nemiah called me his princess and would show me off to his friends and family. There were some people from the country who thought he had kidnapped me, but this wasn't true.

My baby's father Nemiah had a lot of friends who would come by and smoke ganja with him. One evening a friend gave him some ganja to smoke. Shortly after this, he began to say some things that caused me to recognize that he was becoming mad, or crazy. I was so frightened that I called an elderly Rastafarian and relayed the situation to him. He convinced me that Nemiah was, in fact, going mad. He was saying a lot of things that weren't making sense.

He wanted to go into Kingston, so I had no choice but pack a bag and leave with him and the two children. We left behind a house full of antique furniture, which my Aunt Inez had given to me. We didn't know where we were going, but we ended up at a Rasta camp called Bubo Dread, or the Prince Emanuel Rasta camp located on Spanish Town Road. People could just come to this camp and join them. You would get a place to live, but you had to abide by the rules. No woman could live there while having an intimate or sexual relationship with a man, so the brothers lived in separate quarters from the sisters. It was a camp rule. They took their Rasta movement from the Numbers 6, which speaks of not eating vine food, pork, etc.

The camp was also like a shelter and home for a lot of people. The members survived by making brooms to supply all of Jamaica. There was an elderly woman who was in love with the leader, Brother Prince Emanuel, but he wasn't in love with her. He would accept her in order to have his personal needs met. She was very educated and was the sectary of the movement. There was also a younger woman who was also interested in Brother Prince.

There was a sister there who I was close to. She came to the camp with her three children and their father like me and wasn't happy about being separated from him. So we became close friends and shared our problems. We caught one of the sisters coming from Brother Prince's house a couple of nights and realized that they were having a sexual affair. I went and opened my mouth to the wrong source and caused a big outburst. Some brothers and sisters claimed that I was lying. Others knew I wasn't, but they were afraid to say anything, because they feared that they would be asked to leave the camp immediately and would be faced with nowhere to go.

Chapter 12

LIVING IN MAYPEN CEMETERY

By five o'clock in the evening on the day I spoke up about the affair, I was asked to leave the camp. I didn't have anywhere to go, but I decided I wouldn't leave without my son and daughter. I took them not knowing where to go. A madman who lived in an old bus in May Pen Cemetery offered me shelter, so I took the offer. My children's father was still sick in his head and didn't make any attempt to defend me or come after me.

I had been living at the camp for about three years, so I left with just my two children. I was in so much despair that I didn't remember to be fearful about living with a madman in a cemetery. This madman ate from the garbage can. He would offer me food, but I didn't eat any of it. However, I didn't let him know that, because I feared that he would become angry with me. I didn't sleep at nights. He never came near me or tried to make any kind of attempt to force himself on me.

I later learned that this man had belonged to the same Rasta camp and had ended up in a similar situation and was asked to leave. I also learned most of those who were cast out became mad people, so then I was expected to become mad. I did come close to going mad.

Chapter 13

FIGHTING FOR SURVIVAL

One morning I went to get some food for my children, and when I came back, my daughter Princess was missing. Her father had come and taken her. I was devastated, but I had no help to retaliate against the Rasta Camp. Some of the brothers there were very dedicated to the movement. I had to keep quiet, so I moved and went to stay with an old woman who lived alone in a broken-down house. Again, I went to purchase a tin of milk for my son, and when I returned, I found my son missing. His father had come and taken him, leaving me alone.

Losing all of my children hit me so hard that I was mentally affected. I began to go from place to place, not having a home. I couldn't return to my father's house, as my stepmother had made it clear that she didn't want me back there. I had to beg for places to sleep. There was a time when I couldn't get a shower for days or find a place to brush my teeth. I was like a fugitive.

At one point, I heard a voice telling me to try and find a job, so one morning I begged someone to allow me to use their bathroom. I was able to shower without any soap. When I was done, I put on my ragged clothes and went on a job hunt. I was successful. The gentleman who hired me was one of Jamaica's best known criminal lawyers, then, E. K. Brown. It was unbelievable, because it was a filing job, and I thought I wasn't dressed up enough to get the job.

What made it even better was that the man told me that I needed to get to work before anyone else, so he gave me a key to the office. To me, it not only meant that I had a job, but I had somewhere to sleep. I would leave work in the evening and then return at nights. I slept on the floor, got up early, and showered in the bathroom. Soon, I began to look like someone sober. My boss always commended me on how my skin was clean.

He was an excellent lawyer, but he was also full of tricks. He would tell me lies to relay to the clients about their cases. The secretary was his niece, and she became my good friend. One morning before I opened the office, I looked toward the window and saw a man climbing up, as if he was going on the roof. I was very frightened. Then, someone across the road saw him and called the police. Afterward, we found out it was a client who was upset with my boss. He claimed that my boss wasn't handling his case honestly, so he was coming in to shoot and kill all of us.

Chapter 14

MET MY HUSBAND

It was during this time while working with the lawyer E. K. Brown that I met Norman Davis, my husband, who was a singing reggae artist and a member of the Wailing Souls. His group is still performing as strong as ever. They sang backup for Bob Marley and The Wailers. And they also recorded many songs of their own, many of which I had the privilege of listening to in the recording studio.

My husband was also in charge of the Bob Marley Record Shop on Beaston Street. He always sat outside in the evenings where I would have to pass. One evening I stopped and asked him if he could play a song for me. One thing led to another, and we began to talk. I started making it my business to walk pass every evening.

He was already a father of three children by two different mothers—one son and two daughters. I was also a mother of three children—two sons and one daughter. It was then I got to know Bob Marley, who I found to be a jubilant man who loved to make a lot of jokes just to make people laugh. He never liked seeing anyone looking sad. He was very kind to me. My husband and his wife, Rita Marley, grew up together, kind of like cousins. Her aunt, who raised her, was my husband's godmother.

My husband invited me to his house in Trench Town to meet his parents. He told his mother that I was his wife, but his mother asked him how many wives he was going to have. When I looked back on the picture, I realized that he was taking advantage of me, and his mother knew it. He would leave me and not come back until late. He suggested for us to go to a hotel to sleep, because his parents didn't have any accommodation for me to stay. When we went to the hotel, he took advantage of me and had sex with me. We left the hotel in the morning while it was still dark.

I was a stranger to that neighborhood. There were a lot of gunmen and rapists in the area, and my husband walked away, leaving me. I was so scared and was crying, so when I got back to his parents' house, they asked me what was wrong. They both agreed that he shouldn't have left me, knowing how dangerous the area was.

I forgave him and continued with the friendship. But, honestly, I knew he didn't love me. He loved having sex, and I buried my head in the sand and allowed him to. It was in that time that my mother came back to Jamaica from Canada. I found out where she was staying and went to look for her. When I found her, I realized that she had bought all kinds of nice clothes and shoes for my siblings but nothing for me and my eldest sister Shella.

This flung me into the arms of my adversary, and I just thought having sex would take away my problems. He was mean to me and wanted sex from me free of cost. I took him and introduced him to my mother, but she didn't like him because of the community he came from. She constantly told me to get someone else. This, I didn't do, because I was afraid. My husband had a temper. In those days, when a woman broke off of a relationship with a man, she would be beaten badly. I was afraid of that. There were other men who were interested in me, but I never got involved.

I left leave the job with the lawyer E. K. Brown and found myself another job. I also got a chance to meet the great Bob Marley, who used to defend me from my husband. He told me to leave him and said I was a beautiful, black woman. My husband didn't treat me like I was beautiful. He made me feel the opposite, and I began to treat myself the same. I suffered from low self-esteem, and I wasn't myself. His father cried tears sometimes about the way I was treated, but I just kept going back to him. He took the best of me and did plunder.

Then I decided to take the bull by the horns and go back to my father's house instead of bumming around. Before doing so, Bob Marley encouraged us to look at a place. He offered to furnish it for us. Miss Briton, who was Rita Marley's mother, was also assisting us in looking for a place to live. My husband wasn't showing much interest. It never seemed like he wanted to move from his parents' one room, because he seemed quite comfortable.

At that time, my stepmother was doing a live-in job and had my son Michael there with her. I went to her and told her I would like to live at my father's house. Much to my surprise, she was very happy to hand me the keys. I then went there and cleaned up the place. One night I went to Trench Town to look for my husband. He wasn't there, so I decided to wait. It was getting late, but I was determined to see him. I felt like I had to see him. But when he came, he wasn't glad to see me. Instead, he drove me away like a dog. I was ashamed and proceeded to reach for my handbag, which was near his parents. As I was walking, I felt something in my back, like a sharp object, and then I heard a rough voice that said, "Walk."

I became so nervous that I didn't try to look around to see who it was. I just continued walking. He led me to an abandoned building where I was raped at gunpoint. Afterward, he fled the scene. When I got out of the building, I saw quite a few people who looked like they were in shock. They all told me that a rapist normally kills his victims, and they wondered how I wasn't killed.

I got my bag and went and shared what had happened with the other musicians. They were upset with my husband and the way he treated me. Because of that, I decided not to stay over in Trench Town late. I was trying to persuade my husband to come and stay at my father's house, because he didn't have anywhere to accommodate me. I wanted to be happy with him. He was twenty-nine years old, my husband wasn't showing much interest in me sexually or personally. I felt rejected and believed that he was trying to dump me.

I came up with a plan and wrote him a letter telling him that I had gone to the doctor and was told that not having sex was causing me to have headaches. He realized that I might decide to be with someone else, so he decided to come to my father's house. My stepmother didn't have a problem, but she asked if I could make my son Michael come by on the weekends and stay with me. I accepted, not knowing she was having some problems on her job and was planning to leave.

When my stepmother secretly sent my son home one night, my husband made a scene, saying he couldn't stay. Even though it was my father's house, my common-law-husband made my son sleep in the cold night outside. I slept with him outside, and in the morning, my husband sent him back to my stepmother. My son's return caused a big problem for her with her boss, so she became very angry with me.

She blamed me for sending my son back. She pointed out that she was paying the water bill, and my husband wasn't paying any bills. My stepmother was kind to us while we lived there, and every Saturday she would bring food for us. She couldn't understand why my son couldn't stay with me. Of course, I didn't have a problem with my son staying with me, but this man was so hateful. I was so humiliated with the neighbors hearing the uproar. This man would use anything and hit me—whenever, wherever.

My stepmother had to come back to live at my father's house. It was two rooms, so she took one and gave me one. She treated me as her enemy. We used a coal stove to cook and irons that were heated by coals. One day I had fourteen shirts to iron for my husband. I managed to iron thirteen, but one was soiled. I thought that when he came home and saw that thirteen of them were ironed and hung up, he would be happy. Instead, when he came home, he looked and counted them and became very angry, asking for the other one. Before I could open my mouth to explain, he took the dragon stout he was drinking and hit me in the head. The bottle burst in two, and I became unconscious for a while. My stepmother heard, and she came out laughing at me, while I was in tears.

I ran out of the house and hid under the cellar, but my husband came after me. He began to throw huge stones at me. Later, he dragged me out, and because he didn't want me to go to the police, he took me to a bar and gave me some gin to get me drunk. It was a regular thing for him to embarrass me, and this would cause people in the neighborhood to come looking. Some would laugh at me.

When he wanted sex, I couldn't say no. Even if I was hungry, it didn't matter to him. I then became pregnant with my first child for him (my fourth child). My husband's heart was cold, and I was constantly in fear. The beatings continued.

I didn't attend any maternity clinic, and I didn't have any money to purchase baby clothes. I was hungry most of the time, but when I went to Trench Town, Bob Marley would always ask me if I needed food. He would buy me cow foot and beans, telling me that it would make the child strong. In those times, there weren't any ultrasounds to tell the gender of the child, but Bob Marley always told me that I was going to have a boy. I would followed them to the studio and watch them record many of their songs.

My husband walked off his job, despite the fact that he knew I was pregnant. It didn't make much of a difference, though, because he never gave me any money. I can remember being nine months pregnant, carrying a very big stomach, and there was a simple disagreement. My husband took a huge piece of plank and hit me. I went into a shock. My stepmother was not speaking to me, because she was still upset about what my husband had done to my son Michael. I was very afraid of him, and most of my friends were afraid to come around me, because he would insult them. If any of them stopped by for me, they would be constantly watching the gate to run away if they saw him coming. He treated me like a sex machine, and I had to have sex with him three times daily. He didn't care if I wanted to or not.

My son Anthony was born August 11, 1972. I went into the hospital with not much for either myself or my unborn child. This was a great embarrassment, for a woman to go into a hospital to have a baby and not have a bag packed with all the necessary things. In those days, if there was a safe delivery, one would only stay at the hospital for a day. I stayed one day and was discharged. My husband didn't provide cash or a ride, so I had to take a cab. I went down to the Bob Marley Record Shop and got the money from one of Rita Marley's cousins, named Dream, who worked there. He gave me the money so I could pay my cab fare to proceed home.

My stepmother wasn't interested to even look at my son Anthony, and he grew up as such. She was just focused on holding on to my first son, Michael, as if he were her child. I didn't have much to eat most of the time, and I couldn't buy a tin of milk formula, so I resorted to just giving my son Anthony the breast. I breastfed him until I looked like little more than bones. It was so bad that when I walked on the road, some girls would shout at me and call me "mega dog." I felt so ashamed. I didn't look at them or answer them, because that's exactly how I felt, like a mega dog.

My husband didn't wait or give me time to heal before demanding sex. As soon as I came out of the hospital, he insisted on having sex. I couldn't refuse him, fearing he would hit me, so I went along. It was like I was raped, because he didn't care if I was hungry. If my son Anthony woke up to disturb anything, he would become upset with the infant. One night when he demanded sex, my son kept waking up. This kind of made me happy, because I could use my son to get him to stop. Instead, my husband became so furious that he hit the lamp shade off the lamp. It flew off and hit Anthony, cutting him. My husband then ran me out of the house in the dark night, where my son Anthony and I slept outside.

My stepmother heard all of this and asked me what kind of man I am involved with. Then, my stepmother became sick, and despite her malice, I went to her rescue. I took her to the hospital and sought medical attention, and then I took responsibility for her to see that she took her medication. I cleaned her house, cooked her meals, and took care of my son Michael who she held on to as hers. This gave me a little hope of getting food from her, so Anthony could eat. But as soon as she was well, she went back to being her old self.

All this time my husband never purchased a tin of milk formula for our son, but when he turned one, I found a job at Berries Restaurant on East Street, Kingston. I left Anthony with a lady named Miss Smith who I paid on the weekends. I was earning a good salary and was able to provide for my son, Anthony and my husband ate out of it too. He would come and meet me every Friday evening when I got paid. We would go out to a club with a friend and his wife. I paid the bill for me and my common-law—husband, and then on Saturday morning I would give him money so he could go to the market. He said I didn't do a good job of shopping at the market. I was doing well at my job at Berries Restaurant and was offered a position as supervisor. I didn't except the promotion, because there was another girl who believed that she should get it, and I refused.

My boss, who was also the owner of the restaurant, observed how I was doing on the job. One evening he asked me to assist him with some accounts. I found a mistake he had made, so he asked me to assist with checking the day's sales. He discovered that I was good at math and called me into his office quite a few times to assist him. It was then that he offered me the promotion to be supervisor, but I had to refuse it, because another young woman wanted the position. Then he wanted to get close and asked me to become involved with him. I refused, which caused him to become angry. I then left the job.

My common-law-husband encouraged me to take my boss to the Labor Board, but I didn't. I just left. So, I went back to square one—no one working, one child to feed, and nothing coming from the father. I had to go begging for food. As my stepmother watched me and the child go hungry, she never stretched her hand to offer me anything, even though I was there for her when she was sick. Although my husband had stopped working with Bob Marley, he would still go over Trench Town. Some of the time, Bob Marley would ask him to do an errand or two.

At that time, I was pregnant with my fourth child, I felt as if I was lost and in a wonderland. I didn't know what to do, but I was not bitter about being pregnant. I was happy. Again, I didn't get to attend any maternity clinic, so I had to count on my fingers when I would have my baby. My husband was still abusive to me. He would cook whenever there was anything, because he told me I couldn't cook. We never had to pay any bills or rent, because it was my father's house, which was built on a piece of leased land. My stepmother paid the water bill, there was no electricity, and we used kerosene oil lamps, so we were only responsible for our food.

So there I was, unable to feed one child and pregnant with another. I don't know how I survived. On March 13, 1974, I was nine months pregnant. My common-law-husband wasn't there, so I went to visit a friend who was also pregnant. Her baby's father took care of her. He worked and made sure that she was well taken care of.

While I was there, I then began to feel a little pain. It didn't feel serious, because the pain wasn't bad, but I left and went back to my house. I saw some water coming, so I sought the advice of an elderly woman name Miss Smith who told me I shouldn't waste any time. I didn't have anything ready for the hospital, so the woman gave me an old nightgown. I took it and put it in a kind of paper bag. She also gave me $2 to pay the taxi fare, so I left for the hospital. Within a half hour, I gave birth to another daughter Ann-Marie. The hospital had to put clothes on her. I felt like nothing, but I was happy to have my second daughter. I had to undergo a minor surgery, so I was kept in the hospital for three days, after which I was discharged. I had no fare to go home, and my husband didn't come to look for me at the hospital. Someone assisted me with getting a ride.

When I arrived home, my husband wasn't there, so I went in the house, believing he would be happy to see me when he got home. Instead, he was upset and began to quarrel with me about coming home and not cooking anything for him to eat. He was mean, aggressive, and wanted to have sex that same night. My husband wasn't staying with me because he loved me. He had discovered that I might receive some money that had been lingering from my father's estate, and he was watching for the money.

We were all starving for food, and my stepmother wouldn't offer me anything to eat. She had so much food that it was spoiling and she was actually throwing it away. But God showed me a little plan so I could get food for my children. He showed me to go and beg the people who had mango and plum trees to give me some of their fruit, so I could take it to like the school gate and sell them. I did this and was successful. When I was finished, I could purchase food for myself and the children and still have some money for a few other little needs. I sold fruit for a while. While I was out, I would leave the children with my common-law-husband.

It so happened that the owner of the land that my father leased had sold the land to a gentleman in construction. This meant that everyone living on the stretch of land received notice to evacuate. My father's house was the only brick or concrete house, so it couldn't be moved. My stepmother didn't know what to do. The homeowners were planning to take the new land owner to court, but they needed my stepmother to join. Because she had lived there the longest, they would have more power if joined in the lawsuit. They couldn't do anything without her.

But God revealed to me that I should tell her not to join them. I felt that I should approach the man instead and explain what was happening, so that's what I did. The gentleman made me an offer to go and find another piece of land to lease, and he would build me a house. One day I asked my husband to keep the children, so I could look for a piece of land. My husband wasn't worried, because he could go back to his mother's one-room house, but I had to be concerned, because I had my stepmother plus three children.

Despite the fact that my stepmother was being mean, I needed to be there for her. I knew that deep down, she felt disappointed in me at some point with the way this man was behaving. I needed to stand up to the facts and not be ungrateful to her, so I set out one morning to go seek a piece of land. That was when I realized for sure that God was with me. I went to the parish of Bull Bay St. Thomas and I searched with no success. I was ready to walk away and go home when someone asked me what the problem was. Right away I was introduced to a gentleman who had a piece of land to lease. I was directed to where it was, met the owner, and got all the details. I took all of the information back to the man who made me the original offer. He immediately moved to pay for a one-year lease and built me a beautiful, two-bedroom house. He also assisted me with moving and gave me money many times for food. It was like he was rewarding me for encouraging my stepmother to not follow the other tenants' lawsuit.

My stepmother then began to make a fuss, saying she didn't want to move with me. Still, I couldn't leave her. I went back to the man, and he agreed to build her a house also if I found a piece of land for her. I did, and she got a one-bedroom house. I helped her move, so we were living separate places. She insisted on keeping my son, Michael, and I didn't argue. I looked at it as a way to ensure she wouldn't be alone, and he would be there to assist her.

I went back and forth to visit my stepmother and son. But I still missed my other children, Princess and Aaron, who I'd had to leave behind at the Rastafarian camp. Their father held on to them and hid them from me. Most of the time I didn't know where they were, but I was always trying to find them.

My husband found a job after we moved, but he was still mean and abusive. God was good to me. I was living in my own home. But when my husband worked, he had a problem giving me money. He bought the food and did most of the cooking.

I decided to search for my daughter and son and was able to find out that she was at the same Rasta camp. However, the camp had relocated and was actually very close to me. When I went to get my children, their father was unwilling to give them to me. I had to go to the police station, but they told me that it wasn't in their jurisdiction to interfere. The superintendent knew my uncle, who was also in the police force, and offered me help. When he told me he could only assist me to get one of them, I focused on getting my daughter Princess. My intention was to go back at a later time for my son Aaron. He put up a lot of resistance, and the policeman had to use some harsh words to him. Finally, the policeman told me to take the child, so I did.

She was so skinny, and her hair was in locks. Her father deliberately didn't give me any of her clothes, and what she had on was so ragged that I had to stop by a friend's house. She helped us out by giving me a red blouse to put on her. I also borrowed a pair of scissors and trimmed her hair off. I then gave her a bath before taking her home.

I was worried about what my husband would say when he got home, but I was willing to face the consequences. After all, the house was my house, not his. The rest of children were happy when they saw her, especially my son Anthony who stood with me. When my husband came home, he exploded, saying I should take her back to her father. He didn't want her there, but I decided I wouldn't be taking her back, come what may. She slept on the floor that night.

There were many mornings that my husband didn't have bus fare to get to work, and I had to go on the street to beg for money to give him. One morning that I went to beg for bus fare, I asked a man who wanted sex in exchange. He also offered me a single bed, so I took the offer and got the bed and money. I put the bed on my shoulders and took it home. This was for my daughter, so she wouldn't have to sleep on the floor. She and her brother shared it.

Whenever I needed anything, I would go and give this man sex, and he would give me food and money. He was kind to me, lived alone, and was a strong political influence in the community. My husband make it quite clear that he wasn't going to work and support another man's child, even at the point when he wasn't giving much to his own, so I grabbed any kind of job I could find and ran with it. This made me feel independent. The lease on the land was fourteen dollars per year, so I didn't have monthly rent. I bought water from a neighbor, and we used a kerosene oil lamp, so there wasn't an electrical bill.

All this time I'd had to fight life alone without a mother's help. I realized that God was on my side watching over me and talking to me. I knew it was him talking to me, because shortly after my father died, I was outside and found myself just staring up into the skies when I saw like a face of a man. He had on a golden crown. I was so caught up in staring that it happened as if I didn't know where I was. And then I heard Him spoke to me.

He said, "I am your father."

Looking at the face, I knew it wasn't the father who had died. I knew it was the Lord God. I didn't share this with anyone, because I was fearful to do so. Growing up I always heard folks say that no one sees the face of God and lives, even if it's a dream. But I always sensed that I was being watched. I would often look up into the sky and talk, because I believed that God heard me. I knew that He would talk back to me, and I was always successful in the directions He gave me.

Yes, there were times when I felt alone. I felt rejected by my mother most of all and wondered why she hated me. I believed that because my mother rejected me, I would be rejected by everyone, and that was the reason I wasn't loved by these men. I believed that God loved me, and that's why I would look up to the sky and talk to him. I didn't know about praying to him, so I just talked to him.

My Aunt Inez, the one who took me off of the sidewalk, was there for me until the day she died. I went to visit her often. One day when I went to visit I discovered that she was sick. She wasn't someone who loved going to the doctor, so I told her that I'd be back the following day. When I reached her home the next day, there were other tenants in the yard who told me that she had passed away while waiting for me at her front door. Before she died, she told them that everything inside the house was mine. However, I did give some of her things to the folks who assisted her.

I felt so down, but I was encouraged to hear she wasn't angry that I didn't make it in time. At that time I didn't feel alone. My husband was still abusive, but I made myself independent of him with my daughter. I would beg for clothes and then cut them up in order to make clothes for my two daughters. Princess and Ann God was showing me mercy, which I felt, despite everyone who rejected me. I would be okay with just knowing God was there for me. I felt a confidence knowing He would be forever God. I didn't know much about the Bible but was quite sure God loved me. I believed Him, when He told me he would be my father. At this time, I had a two-bedroom house that was very nice and looked good. My husband built a little fence with a gate.

One Sunday morning I was feeling depressed. There wasn't any food, and my husband had a temper. I went to the bathroom and locked the door, but afterward, I heard the voice of God telling me to come out of the yard. I came out as if I didn't see anyone but was just listening to where the Lord was telling me to go. I didn't tell anyone that I was leaving, but I proceeded to the bus stop in Bull Bay where I got on a bus. I didn't have any bus fare, but ask the conductress for a ride, which she gave me.

I had no idea where I was going, but when I reached a stop in Harbour View, I clearly heard the voice of the Lord telling me to get off. After I got off of the bus, I crossed the road and went to the fence of the Sea View Chapel Church. I stood up, as if I were some kind of robot. When a young Syrian man, Michael Mafood, came outside and walked toward me, he asked if I'd like to come inside. I was conscious that my clothes didn't look wonderful, but I accepted the invitation and went inside the church.

The service was already in progress, and I was taken right down to the front. For a moment, I felt a sigh of relief. I felt like someone who had just taken a bath and was feeling so fresh. At the end of the service, I was asked by one of the women if I wanted to give my heart to the Lord. I said that I did, and it was right there and then that I surrendered my life to the Lord Jesus Christ. I'd never felt so much love in all my life. A sister named Joy Bloomfeild took me to her house and gave me clothes and food—so much, in fact, that I couldn't carry it all. When I went home, my children were so happy to see me with so much food. My husband was happy to see the food, but he wasn't happy to hear me say that I'd given my life to the Lord.

Yes, it was true that I had been rejected from the womb by my mother, but I knew for sure that I had been chosen by God. It was all about his timing. I was happy with the difference and knew for sure that God was now my Father, and He wouldn't and couldn't die like my earthly father did. There was a time when I was bitter and angry with God. I didn't understand why he took my father, but the day the voice of God spoke to me from the sky, it didn't matter anymore that my father was dead. I took comfort in the verse in Psalms 27 that says when father and mother forsake me, the Lord will care for me.

Chapter 15

ABUSE OF THE ABUSED

In 1974, I accepted the Lord and was blessed with a wonderful church family who didn't hold back in showing me the love of Christ. They gave me food and clothes. I was very blessed, and my life was changed. I began attending prayer meetings and Bible studies. My husband was upset about me going, despite the help I was receiving. He didn't like to see how the brethren were treating me.

I went to look for my mother and told her that I had become a Christian. She responded by saying that I was going to turn into an old woman, but I couldn't care less. I had somewhere to go.

My common-law-husband would curse me each time I came back from church. One night when I got home from a prayer meeting, I knocked on the door, and my husband opened it. But before I could go inside, he used his fist to punch me in my eye. I felt like I was going to black out. But I didn't let that stop me from going to church. Many times I had to seek refuge from the brothers due to the abuse from my husband. He hit me often in my head and face. He had no love. When the first lease was due for our house, he told me that he wouldn't be paying anything, so I should go look for a man to get it. I went and told one of my church sister Mowatt, and they paid it for me.

I wanted to take my Christian decision a little further and get baptized, but my pastor Milton Davidson advised me that he was unable to do it, because I was living in a common-law relationship. He could only baptize me if we were married. In my mind, that was not possible, because I knew my husband didn't love me. They suggested that they could go to him and explain the situation. If he refused to marry me, he could leave the scene, because the house was mine. I was honestly hoping he would leave, because I was so unhappy.

The neighbors could hear the uproars with the abuse, but he didn't have anywhere to go, so when my pastor and church brethren approached him, he told them that he would do it. However, he said that he didn't have any money for a wedding. I knew he was using that as an excuse, even though I knew he really didn't have the money. The men from my church recognized that it was just an excuse and told him they would finance it. They had him cornered, and he accepted. That was how we got married—the church did everything. But looking back on the wedding, I was not happy. There weren't even any flowers. I didn't tell my mother, because it didn't seem to make any sense to tell her. We were married in 1975, at Sea View Chapel in Harbor View, Kingston, but the abuse continued and got even worse after the wedding.

Later that year, I got pregnant again, but my church family stood up and assisted me while I tried to find work. My husband had a little job, but he wasn't pulling in much money. As always, he was mean to me. Whenever he gave me money, he wanted it to last forever. This pregnancy was different. I was carrying a large stomach, and a lot of people thought I was having twins. The doctors said it was because the baby was breach. I was very frightened, because many mothers lose their lives with a breach pregnancy.

In March 1976, I was nine months pregnant when my husband used his feet to kick me down. God was good to me, though, and I fell on my buttocks. I immediately I went into labor, but my husband didn't care about me being in pain. I rushed to get catch bus. I had no money to pay the bus fare, but I begged for a ride. When I reached my destination, I had to walk two miles in pain to get to the hospital. There were no cell phones then, so I couldn't call any of my brethren. When I arrived at the hospital, I was in so much pain that I could hardly speak to the nurses.

They hurried me to a bed, and some student nurses came to the rescue. I was too frightened to allow them to do anything to me, because I knew the baby was breach. At that moment, one Doctor Mc Donald was on her way out after her shift had ended. She stopped and asked what was wrong. She quickly checked me, said it was an emergency, and quickly called some other top doctors. I was rushed to the operating theater where a caesarean section was performed.

I had another son, Andre. He weighed ten pounds and four ounces. This was my first child who was born in wedlock. The doctors said I wouldn't have been able to have a natural delivery. They also advised me that having more children would kill me.

I asked someone to call one of my church brothers. They all rushed to the hospital, and I was well taken care of. My husband never had the heart to say he was sorry. I wasn't in need of anything, and my children weren't either.

My mother wasn't there for me, and she was always the same. I was her rejected daughter; she couldn't have cared less, but I always went to look for her. Before going in her house, I had to gear myself up for some kind of cursing. She had helped my other sister with her child, but she didn't provide anything for my children. She told me that she wouldn't be offering me any help, because she didn't like the man I was with. She always found excuse after excuse. She couldn't love me or treat me like the rest of siblings. I was her rejected child.

I visited my stepmother from time to time, and she, too, was quite comfortable in the house that I helped her get. She was much more pleasant to me that she had been in the past and would offer me anything she could. But things were different, because I was living in my own house.

I had Christian brothers and sisters who loved me so much that they made sure that I was never in need of anything. My church family had to come to my house many times and put their feet down about the abuse from my husband. One of them got him a better job as a night watchman. He was earning a little more, but he was still being mean. He then began to help me out with the children, including my daughter who wasn't his. He would cook most of the time, because he said I wasn't a good cook.

Things began to change with the interception of the church family, which included people of all different races. It was about loving one other. They saw to it that I wasn't out of food. The abuse also changed. It was still there, but my husband was afraid that my church family would call the cops or encourage me to ask him to leave. My mother-in-law as in my husband mother became jealous of my house, because she believed that her son had built it for me. One time she came over to tell him that she needed somewhere to live as well. She was upset, but I didn't tell her the house was mine. She had preferred his first woman, who was the mother of his first two children. But my father-in-law was different. He would argue about the abusiveness. He and his father didn't get along much, but he was much closer to his mother.

Chapter 16

LANDLORD WANTED SEX

The man whom we were leasing the land from began to come by my house when my husband was at work. He suggested that we begin a sexual relationship and that he could come on the days my husband was gone. He told me that he had the same arrangement with some of his other tenants, but I refused. He was upset with me, so I relayed the matter to one of my church sisters, who suggested that we should take the matter up in prayer. After finding out about what had happened with this man, a church brother Grier offered me two acres of land in Harbour View. My husband didn't show any interest, but I accepted the offer. My brethren helped me build a little one-room board house. My husband never knew where it was until the very day we were moving. After we moved, I sold the one I had, so we were out of Bull Bay.

Chapter 17

LIFE CHANGED

Harbour View was a much more residential community than where we had lived in Bull Bay. I was also closer to my church and didn't need to take a bus. My church brethren were also closer, as most of them lived in the same community. My husband was a little more loving, so we decided to do a little farming on the property, along with his night job and me selling snacks to the children at the Harbour View Primary School gate. I would sell off all my goods in no time and leave to purchase more, which would also sell off quickly. Things were getting better. The church brethren were friends to my husband, and my husband was living in a residential community for the first time.

My husband got my eldest daughter in Harbour View Primary School; the others were not quite ready for school. I had four children with me, and I was doing fine. We were no longer hungry or in need of clothes. God had been good to me. Some of my brethren were nurses, teachers, lawyers, doctors, pastors, and other types of professionals. The things my mother told me to make me feel bad were no longer affecting me, because during this time, she was living in a rented house. I still went to visit her and my siblings. She didn't want them to come at my house. My eldest sister, Shella, who also felt rejected because she thought our mother didn't want her, was now living in Kingston with her common-law-husband. She was very hardworking, and we had a good relationship, because we comforted each other. Some weekends she and her husband would come and spend the weekend with me, and she would cook dinner for us. We were both doing much better than our siblings, which made our mother furious. She cursed us, saying we were a disgrace. Because we both sold food to earn money, she looked down on us, but we were independent. My sister and her husband bought a house in the Portmore Kingston Jamaica, where she is still living. My mother didn't love her either, but the aunt who raised her treated her like a daughter instead of a niece.

My life changed, and I was not the same anymore. I was feeling independent, but we were the only family living in our area of Harbour View. My safety became a concern for one of my church sisters, because she knew my husband worked nights, leaving me and the children home alone. She suggested that I look somewhere else to live, and I agreed because it was very terrifying there at night.

Chapter 18

THINGS GETTING BETTER

My church sister struck a golden discovery. There was a job opening at Ardenne High School; they needed a live live-in caretaker. We wasted no time, and my husband got the job. With came a house with two bedrooms, a living room, kitchen, bathroom, and patio where the children could play.

I sold the one-bedroom house in Harbour View and used the money to pay for the move. A church sister Mowatt took me and bought us some furniture. It was like moving into heaven. In Harbour View, we had to shower with the hose outside, and we cooked outside, but it felt much better that living in Bull Bay.

After the move, things started to get better. My husband was now the caretaker for Ardenne High School, which was one of Jamaica's best high schools. The salary was the best in his life. Plus, we didn't have to pay for rent, electricity, water, or phone, because all of those things were benefits of the job.

I decided to find something to do and came up with selling things from my kitchen to the school children. I started with three boxes of donuts per day and went up to seventy-five boxes per day. Out of my little business, I was able to get my eldest daughter Princess into Ardenne Prep School.

My husband wore a uniform with a blue short-sleeve shirt and dark blue pants. Things changed for him. He was a little bit more loving, and the abuse stopped. God was so good, and I had my own little business.

My mother was never pleased with anything I did, but I invited my little brother to come and visit me, and I would give him money. My sister Elaine who lived with my mother came from time to time to borrow money, but I wouldn't lend anything to her. Instead, I gave her what she needed. By this time, my two white sisters had migrated to the United States and visited our mother from time to time. I didn't hear much from them and didn't have any address, so I couldn't write to them. But I was okay and busy trying to take care of my family.

Through the success of my little business, I was making per day what my husband was making per week. I was able to send my three children to Ardenne Prep School, which was expensive, but I wanted to give them the best. They were always well taken care of.

I was also able to afford an assistant to help out with the housework. My eldest daughter and I weren't able to keep up with the housework, which is something I inherited from my father.

I went from the sidewalk to being able to afford to employ someone. I was even able to return help to a few of my church sisters who were there for me, and I also helped many more. I was blessed by the Lord Jesus Christ of His mercy day by day. I was loved and respected by most of the teachers there.

Even though I had been rejected from the womb, I was chosen by God.